We Are Going To Be Parents

The journey to becoming Mom and Dad.
A pregnancy writing journal.

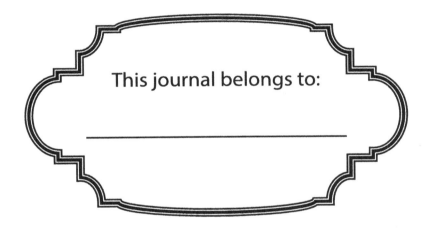

This journal belongs to:

_____

What Is Included:

A notebook and journal designed for parents expecting a baby soon. Included are pages where you can record details of your journey, list baby names, reflect on a month to month and just write down all your experiences so you can share and save your memories.

Lets Get Started

Exepcted Due Date: _____

Actual Due Date: _____

Contacts
Doctors, Emergency Contact, Family etc.

Name: _____ Phone: _____
Address:_____
Relationship:_____ Email: _____

Name: _____ Phone: _____
Address:_____
Relationship:_____ Email: _____

Name: _____ Phone: _____
Address:_____
Relationship:_____ Email: _____

Name: _____ Phone: _____
Address:_____
Relationship:_____ Email: _____

Insurance Information
Company: _____
Policy Details: _____
Cover Details: _____
Address: _____
Contact: _____
Email: _____
Website: _____

Hospital Packing List

Journey to Becoming Pregnant
Express the experience of finding out about the pregnancy.

_____

_____

_____

_____

_____

_____

_____

_____

_____

_____

_____

_____

_____

_____

_____

_____

Baby Names

Boy Names: Girl Names:

_____   _____

_____   _____

_____   _____

_____   _____

_____   _____

_____   _____

_____   _____

_____   _____

_____   _____

_____   _____

_____   _____

_____   _____

_____   _____

_____   _____

_____   _____

_____   _____

_____   _____

Month One ~ Thoughts and Reflections

Month Two ~ Thoughts and Reflections

Month Three ~ Thoughts and Reflections

Month Four ~ Thoughts and Reflections

Month Five ~ Thoughts and Reflections

Month Six ~ Thoughts and Reflections

Month Seven ~ Thoughts and Reflections

Month Eight ~ Thoughts and Reflections

Month Nine ~ Thoughts and Reflections

Month Ten ~ Thoughts and Reflections

Month Eleven ~ Thoughts and Reflections

Made in the USA
Las Vegas, NV
27 January 2023

66367199R00066